Michael Rosen's SAD BOOK

words by

Michael Rosen

pictures by

Quentin Blake

WALKER BOOKS

AND SUBSIDIARIES

LONDON · BOSTON · SYDNEY · AUCKLAND

This is me being sad.
Maybe you think I'm being happy in this picture.
Really I'm being sad but pretending I'm being happy.
I'm doing that because I think people won't
like me if I look sad.

Sometimes sad is very big.
It's everywhere. All over me.

Then I look like this.
And there's nothing I can do about it.

What makes me most sad is when I think
about my son Eddie. He died. I loved him
very, very much but he died anyway.

Sometimes this makes me really angry.
I say to myself, "How dare he go and die like that?
How dare he make me sad."

He doesn't say anything,
because he's not there any more.

Sometimes I want to talk about all this to someone.
Like my mum. But she's not here any more either. So I can't.
I find someone else. And I tell them all about it.

Sometimes I don't want to talk about it.
Not to anyone. No one. No one at all.
I just want to think about it on my own.
Because it's mine. And no one else's.

Sometimes because
I'm sad I do crazy
things – like shouting
in the shower ...

banging a spoon
on the table ...

or making my cheeks go whooph,
boooph, whooph.

Sometimes because I'm sad I do bad things.
I can't tell you what they are.
They are too bad. And it's not fair on the cat.

Sometimes I'm sad and I don't know why.
It's just a cloud that comes along and covers me up.
It's not because Eddie's gone.
It's not because my mum's gone. It's just because.

Maybe it's because things now aren't like they were a few years ago.
Like my family. It's not the same as it was a few years ago.
So what happens is that there's a sad place inside me
because things aren't the same.

I've been trying to figure out ways of being sad that
don't hurt so much. Here are some of them:

I tell myself that everyone has sad stuff.
I'm not the only one. Maybe you have some too.

Every day I try to do one thing I can be proud of.
Then, when I go to bed, I think very, very, very
hard about this one thing.

I tell myself that being sad isn't the same
as being horrible. I'm sad, not bad.

Every day I try to do one thing that means
I have a good time. It can be anything so long
as it doesn't make anyone else unhappy.

And sometimes I write about sad.

Where is sad?
Sad is anywhere.
It comes along and finds you.

When is sad?
Sad is any time.
It comes along and finds you.

Who is sad?
Sad is anyone.
It comes along and finds you.

I write:

Sad is a place
that is deep and dark
like the space
under the bed

Sad is a place
that is high and light
like the sky
above my head

When it's deep and dark
I don't dare go there

When it's high and light
I want to be thin air.

This last bit means that I don't want to be here.
I just want to disappear.

But sometimes I find myself looking at things:
people at a window ...

a crane and a train full of people going past.

And then I remember things:
my mum in the rain ...

Eddie walking along the street,
laughing and laughing and laughing.

Doing his old man act in the school play.

Us playing saves on and off the sofa.

And birthdays ... I love birthdays.

Not just mine – other people's as well.

Happy birthday to you ... and all that.

And candles.

There must be candles.

First published 2004 by Walker Books Ltd
87 Vauxhall Walk, London SE11 5HJ

This edition published 2008

2 4 6 8 10 9 7 5 3 1

Text © 2004 Michael Rosen
Illustrations © 2004 Quentin Blake

This book has been typeset in Bookman

Printed in China

British Library Cataloguing in Publication Data:
a catalogue record for this book is
available from the British Library.

ISBN 978-1-4063-1316-1

www.walkerbooks.co.uk